Contents

HAPPY HOUR? WAIT
I WANT TO GO!
I JUST NEED A LITTLE
HELP WITH THESE
EXTRA REPORTS...
IN
REPORT
ACG

Chapter 1: Entitlement

If there is a consistent criticism of recent college graduates today, it is that they have an unbearable sense of entitlement: an expectation that, on the job, they will experience a certain amount of respect, praise, happiness, freedom, and personal time. Jon Krakauer in his book *Into the Wild* described this phenomenon best – "It is easy, when you are young, to believe that what you desire is no less than what you deserve, to assume that if you want something badly enough, it is your God-given right to have it." A more realistic expectation is that you are entitled to nothing; you must earn everything.

A number of my students over the years have prided themselves on the value of their soon-to-be-earned degrees. I can appreciate their sense of dignity; after all, I chose to work at their universities premeditatedly and continue to serve as an academic instructor with tremendous honor. These students leave the demure domain of pride and enter the reprobative realm of entitlement when they expect that recruiters will be flooding their email inboxes with escalating offers of employment and signing bonuses. Regardless of the quality, expense, or reputation of one's alma mater, a degree does not make a man – his attitude, conscientiousness, and willpower does.

When I began my career as a young lawyer, I can recall asking the managing partner of my office for information about compensation. I wanted to know when I would receive a raise – specifically whether the timing of my raise would be tied to my beginning date of employment or the calendar year. And, in conformity with my legal training, which favored the written over the spoken word, I delivered this question along with other, related questions in the form of an email. (If you – the reader – are not cringing right now, you must understand why you should be.) His response was radio silence.

Before you commence your first job, you should flesh out the material terms and conditions of employment. You should receive and review a contract that contains, at the very least, details about your salary and benefits, job title and description, expected work hours, and term of work (if any). Do not be afraid to ask for details that are not initially supplied to you. After receiving satisfactory answers to your questions and the execution of your employment contract, you must absolutely adhere to the principle that a deal is a deal. Do not begin employment and thereafter attempt to negotiate for greater pay, lesser hours, or more substantial vacation time.

In my case, I was not trying to bargain for more than I had originally agreed, but I was (in legalese) attempting to prosecute the answer to an interrogatory which should have been propounded in advance of signing my contract of employment. Post hoc wisdom informs me that I should have asked a colleague or affable superior about the timing of the firm's raises rather than the most powerful person in my office. Moreover, I should never have placed a topic as ethereal as compensation in the form of an email. In-person communications, especially through informal channels such as lunches or happy hours, are a much better avenue for asking sensitive questions. They also allow eminently important non-verbal behavior to be on display: facial expressions, eye contact, and touching, which often convey more information about one's feelings and level of comfort than does the written or spoken word.

In my mid-twenties, I struggled to understand the difference between courtesy and respect. Boiled down to its essence, the difference between these two concepts is a matter of display. Courtesy is always displayed externally. It refers to one's social behavior. A person who is courteous demonstrates good manners and is considered to be socially polite. Courtesy does not need to stem from authentic feelings. One can be courteous to another without having any feelings of admiration or attraction towards him or her. Respect, on the other hand, comes from within. It is a sense of appreciation one person has for another on the basis of one or more qualities, characteristics, or actions taken. The recipient of one's respect may, unfortunately, never know he or she has received it.

Respect can never be brought about by request. It can only be achieved through unrelenting effort, consistency, and high moral conduct.

You must understand that your receipt of courtesy from another individual does not always mean that you possess his or her respect. The practical significance of this distinction lies in the following workplace phenomenon: young professionals too often believe that they are more highly regarded by their superiors than actuality. This presupposition of respect lends itself to a young professional's sense of entitlement, which serves only to lower the amount of respect the superior has for the young professional. This dangerous, downward spiral for the young professional can be avoided by understanding that outward displays of courtesy bear potentially no resemblance to their proponents' inward beliefs.

What was stated above is worth repeating: you must earn everything. Ask yourself whether you earned the courteous treatment received. If you accomplished something material and availed your company or supervisor thereby, then that outward display of courtesy may actually be consistent with an inward feeling of respect. If you did not, then you should assume that the courteous display is demonstrative of good social etiquette and nothing more.

Chapter 2: Trying To Be A Leader Too Soon

From a psychological standpoint, humans often associate age with wisdom. More years means more time for a person to have accumulated a posteriori knowledge and social finesse. Comparatively, in the animal kingdom, the eldest elephant is the leader of its parade; a silverback gorilla, typically at least 12 years of age, makes nearly all of the decisions for its troop; elder female sperm whales, sometimes referred to as "sages," lead their pods, which can consist of females of all ages and younger males; and adult Broad-winged Hawks often are the lead birds in their flocks, flying in front of juveniles. With the possible exception of change-based leadership, young and seasoned professionals alike will deny a young person a role in leadership.

When I began my career, I came on to the scene with both arms swinging. As is true for all young lawyers and educators, my knowledge of law practice and curriculum development was far from exhaustive; but I demonstrated no shortage of creativity, effort, and passion. In addition thereto, I attempted to lead. I believed that I had some uncommon skills, unique among my colleagues, and – in fact – I did; nonetheless, some of my enterprising attempts backfired. Some of the true leaders of one or more of my places of business rejected me. They let me know and feel my position of inferiority. I was the proverbial outstanding nail, in Japanese culture, that was hammered down.

It is extraordinarily difficult to be a young leader. Definitionally, unless a person believes that he is a leader of himself, a leader must have followers. In the workplace, seniority and tenure, though not as robustly influential as in generations past, predominate over youth and inexperience. In short, your established coworkers are not interested in having you attempt to lead them, and they will not follow you if you try.

I would never stifle or disincentivize creativity, effort, or passion. All of these things are good. Young persons often – mistakenly – place leadership in the same category. Leadership, instead, is a horse of a fundamentally different color. Like fine wine, the value of leadership increases over time. Unlike fine wine, unaged leadership is repugnant. It is perceived poorly – arousing disapprobation and discontent amongst those who have earned their positions of leadership as well as those who are laying the foundation for their ascension to leadership.

Rather than attempt to lead at the outset of your career, you should spend a minimum of three years learning your craft and fostering sponsorship from your superiors. Ingratiate yourself with them. Do not brown-nose, flatter, or fawn over them, or resort to Machiavellian means. Do mimic them, be generally agreeable with them, and laugh at their jokes. By the end of your initiation period, the timing of which is dependent upon the turnover rate in your industry and size of your specific company, the company will have employees more youthful than you (who will naturally look up to you), and your superiors will begin to give your positions credence.

Wring the most out of inhabiting one of the lower rungs of your company's totem pole. You have much to learn. Never in your career will your mistakes be less costly. Ask more questions than you give answers. Listen more than you speak. Immerse yourself in books about organizational behavior and leadership. Once you have reached the end of your industry's equivalent of a residency period, it is time to gracefully peel off the kid gloves and begin to take charge.

Chapter 3: Lack Of Follow-Through

Nothing will cause more damage to your personal and professional life than losing your trustworthiness. Dishonesty is a common culprit for a loss of trust. Once trust is lost, it is very, very hard to earn back.

Abraham Lincoln is quoted to have said the following: "No man has a good enough memory to make a successful liar." He was right. All liars will eventually be caught. While it may be difficult, at times, to be honest, you will live a simpler, cleaner, more manageable life if you do.

There is a form of dishonesty that is exceedingly common in the workplace today. It engenders a loss of trust, as does all dishonesty, and violently pins the credibility of its proponent against the front gates of a one-way graveyard. The more frequently it is repeated, the more successful its proponent is in opening the perilous gates to a reputation's ultimate resting place. What is this ubiquitous form of dishonesty? It is a lack of follow-through.

The Bible, in Proverbs 25:14, describes this form of dishonesty beautifully: "Like clouds and wind when no rain follows is the man who boastfully promises what he never gives." Since biblical times, clouds and wind have been perceived as a promising sign of rain. Farmers need rain to nurture their crops, which ultimately feed their families and their communities. Particularly before modern meteorology, even a single incident of cloudiness and windiness without rain would cause disappointment. Multiple occurrences, however, could be devastating. Likewise, a modern man who makes a commitment and thereafter breaches it runs the risk of losing his credibility. If he does so often, he has single-handedly, through a collection of scanty tugs, unplugged his ventilator – his reputation's last connection to life support – and, with the same hand, tapped the final nail in its coffin.

I have never struggled with honesty as it is customarily understood. It was not until I got so busy juggling projects of various shapes and sizes that I could not meet all of the expectations placed upon me. Clients made demands on me. Partners, shareholders, and department chairs made demands on me. My family and friends made demands on me. And, more important than all of the former demands, I made demands on myself. How could I satisfy all of these competing demands? I could not. There were not enough hours in the day. When I came to this realization, at first, I was not sure how to handle it. Who would be the victim? In other words, who would I choose to disappoint? Among the demanders, who would be the most forgiving? Regrettably, I chose me. I sacrificed my happiness and even my mental and physical health so that I could satisfy all the other demanders.

What could I have done – and what can you do – to avoid this mistake? To begin with, do not make false promises. Do not say that you will get something done or complete a task by a certain time if you know that you will not. You will lose what I have told you is so difficult to gain back – trust. On the other hand, do not sacrifice yourself. If you are not taking care of yourself, nobody else will. Your magic bullet is to learn when to say "No." Certain tasks, projects, or events can wait. They do not have to be done immediately, especially when there are actually urgent tasks to which you must tend.

To say no, I must admit, you need courage. Courage is a sine qua non for success.

If you do not have the courage to say "No," or you fear that saying so could be interpreted poorly, here are three other options.

First, state that you will try your hardest to get the assignments done by their respective deadlines but that you, despite working extra hours, foresee potential for failure. If you are subsequently questioned, explain your rationale; but be brief in so doing. Your boss will not look fondly upon an explanation as to why you cannot timely achieve a certain task when you have wasted valuable time delivering said explanation.

Second, ask your boss to prioritize your projects. When asking for this prioritization, concisely explain that you want to accomplish all of the projects assigned you but need to ensure the most important ones are timely completed. This tacitly places your boss on notice that not all of the projects may be completed by their deadlines.

Third, and probably the most consequential of this lot, learn and eventually attempt to master the art of delegation. Have a person or two in the pipeline whom you can count on to assist you in times of need. Be prepared to reciprocate for him or her. This technique will potentially allow you to complete all tasks without having to let any person down.

The late Edward Rickenbacker, America's most successful fighter ace in World War I, provides an excellent, executive summary for this chapter: "I can give you a six-word formula for success: 'Think things through – then follow through.'"

Chapter 4: Putting Your Career In Your Boss's Hands

There is no other person in this world who cares more about your career advancement than you. Let me state that another way for the sake of emphasis: if you want to succeed, you must take personal responsibility for your success; you cannot rely upon your boss or anybody else to bring it to you.

You may have heard of the term "paternalistic corporation." To what does that term refer? It refers to a corporation that does business on the basis of what it believes to be good for its employees without regard for the opinions of the employees. Some have stated that this type of corporation is extinct. I am not one of them. I believe that it is less common than it once was but that it still exists.

Between the extremes of personal and corporate selfishness exists a middle-ground in which all people beginning their careers should seek to position themselves. Envision this middle-ground as the intersection, within the famous John Venn diagram, of your corporation's circle of interest and your own circle of interest. It is where you are true to yourself, capturing all personal advancement, and are loyal and obedient to your company.

At least once a year you can expect to be reviewed by your boss or by a committee of which your boss is a member. This will provide helpful feedback to you – you will learn where you stand in relation to the company's expectations. Do not allow this review to unilaterally dictate your behavior. Remember, the feedback you receive in your review represents the corporation's circle of interest.

After receiving this review, you should conduct your own, personal review. Measure your progress against your defined objectives, which exist within your circle of interest. The overlap between your company's expectations and your own objectives – represented by the intersection of your Venn diagram – should be your highest focus. Spend your choicest quality energy on these bilateral objectives. Do not neglect the remainder of your circle, and do not neglect the remainder of your company's circle either; but keep your emphasis on achieving the shared objectives.

Your boss, most likely, is not your mentor. Do not ever assume that your boss is mentoring you. You must secure a personal mentor, who is a professional advisor or coach. She need not be an employee of your company, but it can be helpful if she is. She should be a person whom you respect and perceive as successful. Those feelings should be closely reciprocated – she ought to respect you and perceive you as a rising star.

Your mentor can give you candid, unbiased feedback. Your boss cannot. Your mentor does not need you to satisfy company expectations and does not have any money (instead, merely her gratuitous time) invested in you. Nearly everything a true mentor tells you will inure to your benefit, not your company's or even hers. Your boss may even be legally prohibited from serving in this capacity, even if he wanted to, because of the application of fiduciary law: he owes the company duties of care, loyalty, and good faith; he must act in the best interest of the company. To the extent your interests and the company's collide, your boss may legally be pressured to side with the company's.

If you place full faith in the busy hands of your boss, you probably will overlook what they are not showing you – your company's tea leaves. Companies rise and fall. Divisions thereof are spawned and aborted. If you do not step out from behind your boss' shadow and expose yourself to the winds of change, you may find yourself discreetly coddled within the eye of the storm.

As a related word of caution, understand that – unless the company stands to benefit – your boss will not recommend that you depart and go under the employ of another company. This is a decision that you, hopefully with the input of your mentor, will have to make. Transitions from one company to another take time, though, and you do not know when a better opportunity could arise. For that reason, be sure to keep your resume current. I would advise updating it as frequently as once a month.

Chapter 5: Specializing Too Early

The dichotomy between specialists and generalists is often overblown in academic circles, but it deserves your attention. Are you better off becoming a specialist or a generalist? It is a question of depth versus breadth. Specialists lack breadth, but they have significant depth in their area of expertise. Generalists lack depth, but they have significant breadth across the areas of their disciplines. Let us take a closer look.

Specialists can ordinarily charge more than generalists. Within the medical profession, a primary care physician makes, on average, between $160,000 and $200,000 per year. A specialized physician makes, on average, between $275,000 and $300,000 per year. Using rough numbers, thus, we know that a specialized physician makes fifty percent more than a primary care physician. Other examples of the compensation disparity between specialists and generalists abound.

Remember the quote often attributed, potentially erroneously, to Mark Twain: "There are three kinds of lies: lies, damned lies, and statistics." The above compensation information fails to take into account a deluge of considerations favoring generalists. Let us examine four of them.

First, generalists are able to market their services to a larger audience. They have offerings that are of use to a greater number of people. Upon building large client or customer bases, generalists have the opportunity to scale their businesses. In other words, with the goal of making more money, they can hire associates to perform the work they previously undertook and thereby earn more money than they could independently.

Second, generalists have broader peripheral knowledge. They are able to take a holistic approach to their service models, factoring in tangential items that are difficult to sever from the subject matter. In today's interconnected global economy, this could mean expanding one's analysis from North American and European markets to include the "BRIC" countries – Brazil, Russia, India, and China.

This second point merits additional analysis. Have you ever met a person with an undergraduate business degree from Harvard, Yale, Columbia, Brown, Dartmouth, or Stanford? If you have, he was probably riding on a unicorn with red phoenixes perched on each of his shoulders. Yes, he looked that ridiculous because he was merely a figment of your imagination. Those schools, as well as others, do not offer undergraduate business degrees. While their individual reasons may vary, common, aggregated explanations provided are that the schools want their students to be taught rather than trained and to receive a more well-rounded education. The most selective schools in the world, therefore, explicitly encourage the materialization of generalists. (Note, however, that while the author agrees with the concept of a broad and diversified education, he does not agree that this end cannot be satisfied by pursuing and obtaining an undergraduate business degree.)

Third, generalists are not subject to the ultimate downfall of specialists – potential extinction. The knowledge, skills, or abilities that make a specialist unique may become obsolete. Generalists can simply cease offering a service that has been rendered useless by the passage of time and continue offering those with market value.

Fourth, generalists are able to dip their toes in the water without getting all the way in. If the water is too hot or too cold, generalists can remove their toes and find water more pleasing to them. Relatedly, they are able to determine, through experimentation, the stroke or strokes in which they excel. After trying the breaststroke, backstroke, butterfly, and freestyle, a generalist may learn that he simply cannot swim as well on his back compared to on his stomach. Had this person pursued the specialist route, he may have not only entered into uncomfortable waters but also attempted to propel himself in a comparatively inefficient manner.

Within the legal profession, I have seen an uncanny amount of law students and young attorneys make the mistake of focusing on merely one or two areas of law. Why are they doing this? Like specialized physicians, specialized lawyers are able to charge more per hour. Law students and young attorneys are doing their best to follow the money. You can now understand why these prematurely specialized attorneys may (1) have smaller client bases and difficulty scaling, (2) fail to see the forest for the trees with respect to complex, interwoven legal issues, (3) become unemployable in the event of a major shift in the law, or (4) be unhappy in their work and leaving talent on the table.

This chapter is not meant to discourage you from becoming a specialist. We need specialists, and, again, specialists can be compensated handsomely. This chapter is meant to discourage you, however, from becoming a specialist before the opportunity is ripe. Immerse yourself in the gamut of offerings within your field, and you will enjoy more perspective than a pure specialist could ever imagine.

Chapter 6: Emotional Unintelligence

We all are familiar with the term "intelligence quotient," abbreviated as "IQ." This is a measure of a person's cognitive abilities, in relation to his age group, derived after completion of one or more standardized tests. Most people are much less familiar with the terms "emotional intelligence" or "emotional quotient", abbreviated as "EI" or "EQ."

Emotional intelligence is the capacity of an individual to recognize his and other people's emotions (subcategorized as emotional awareness), to discriminate between and correctly identify feelings, and to self-regulate his emotions and manage the emotions of other people. High emotional intelligence is often positively correlated with better social relationships, better family and intimate relationships, better professional relationships, and better psychological well-being.

In all but a few types of jobs, your emotional intelligence will make or break you. Having high emotional intelligence can mean the difference between being promoted and stagnating or retaining your job and getting fired. High emotional intelligence translates into successful networking lunches during the day, happy hours after work, and marriages when you return home for the evening.

Before I tell you how to build your emotional intelligence, I need to explain what mistakes I typically see concerning it. There are three of them. The first is newly employed people focusing too much on the technical aspects of their job. Eager to learn and become competent, these people fail to understand the immense importance of first impressions. The old adage is true – you only have one chance to make a first impression. When you arrive at your place of employment, your coworkers and superiors will be (whether you like it or not) making snap judgments about you. There will be no deliberating.

The second mistake is newly employed people spending too much time on their computers and other devices. We only have twenty-four hours in a day. Twelve of those hours, at most, are spent at the workplace. If you have managed to stay within your office or cubicle for the majority of that time, you have barred yourself from communicating with people in person. Your emotional intelligence will wane without human interaction.

The third mistake relates to the second – newly employed people attempt to substitute social media interaction for in-person interaction. Social media skills are in demand, but they are no replacement and do not provide good training for live, face-to-face communications. Until pulling out your phone and using it to display an emoji representative of your present feelings becomes socially acceptable, you will need to learn how to express yourself and how to read the expressions of other people. I have seen young people so entrenched in electronic communication that, when I attempt to engage them in conversation, I could mistake them for high-quality wax models positioned upright in a modern natural history museum.

Now that you have been apprised of three of the most common emotional intelligence mistakes made in the workplace, let me tell you how to rid yourself of them. With regard to first impressions, you need to understand that the quality of your work is almost irrelevant. First impressions are made almost instantly. By the time your first piece of work is reviewed, your colleagues' opinion of you will have been nearly fully formed. To make a good first impression, you need to focus on your personal appearance, hygiene, and overall presentation. I am not telling you that you need to change the way that you look. You simply need to look like the best version of yourself. Make sure that your hair is trimmed, clean, and styled professionally. Smell nicely – wear deodorant and a soft fragrance, but do not apply too much. Give a firm handshake. Keep proper posture: do not slouch, for it may give the impression that you lack confidence. Be sure to smile; in that same vein, be sure that you have recently brushed your teeth or used mouthwash. Make good eye contact – it shows interest. Dress well, and do not wear wrinkled clothes or scuffed shoes.

With regard to spending too much time in your office, try walking down the hall to talk with your colleague rather than sending her an email. Instead of picking up the phone to speak with your assistant, ask her to meet you in a mutually convenient conference room. When you are taking a break, find a few others who are as well. Eat lunch, or even just a snack, with them. Better yet, ask a colleague to take a short, ten-minute walk with you during the day. Not only will this help you build a genuine relationship, but your body and mind will thank you as well.

With regard to spending too much time on social media, learn to redirect your energies. Your mind is telling you that relationships and interaction are good, so use this evolutionary psychology-based urge productively – get a cup of coffee with a friend, strike up a conversation with a new person at the gym, or get to know your neighbors.

Other foundational ways to improve your emotional intelligence are working on your listening skills, trying to maintain composure under pressure, thinking before reacting, steering yourself away from conflict, and, as the expression goes, trying to place yourself in the other's shoes.

Businesses, large or small, are comprised of people. It is these people, and your ability to get along with them, that will determine the success or failure of the enterprise and your career. While entities may be distinct from their owners and employees, such distinction is one of a legal nature only. Ignore feelings, emotions, and relationships at your peril.

I will conclude this chapter with an outstanding quote from Dr. Daniel Goleman's best-selling book, *Emotional Intelligence*: "Much evidence testifies that people who are emotionally adept – who know and manage their own feelings well, and who read and deal effectively with other people's feelings – are at an advantage in any domain in life, whether romance and intimate relationships or picking up the unspoken rules that govern success in organizational politics."

Chapter 7: Surrounding Yourself With The Wrong People

If you have never read *How To Win Friends & Influence People* by Dale Carnegie, then, by all means, put this book down and pick up Mr. Carnegie's book. It is one of the best, if not the best, self-help books ever written. Within it, Carnegie quotes La Rochefoucauld, one of the 17th century's most influential French philosophers, as having said the following: "'If you want enemies, excel your friends; but if you want friends, let your friends excel you.'"

The Bible, in Proverbs 13:20, teaches us the following lesson: "Walk with the wise and you become wise, but the companion of fools fares badly." Jim Rohn, a famous motivational speaker, said "You are the average of the five people you spend the most time with." Keith Ferrazzi in *Never Eat Alone* wrote "We are the people we interact with." Even the advice of dieticians can be loosely lumped together with the aforementioned pearls of wisdom: "You are what you eat."

Could Rochefoucauld, Carnegie, the Bible, Rohn, Ferrazzi, and dieticians all be wrong? Yes, they could; but they are not. You are who you associate with. Walk, talk, eat, laugh, and work with successful people.

A common mistake I see among young people is that they tend to spend time with people who make them feel comfortable. Similar to comfort foods, these comfort eliciting people are not necessarily good for you.

Typically, these people are "friends" from high school or college. After you enter the working world, you may not have much in common with them. They may be more interested in reliving moments of a day gone by than focusing on advancing their lives or careers. (This is not always the case, of course. I consider myself very fortunate to have sterling friends who I met as early as elementary school.)

As a young professional, regardless of the caliber of your old friends, you need to spend more of your free time meeting new people. You should be volunteering for charities, participating in leadership programs, attending networking events, joining recreational sports teams, and congregating with fellow subscribers of your religion. Irrespective of the type of activity, you should be engaging with people with whom you share common interests.

In addition to surrounding yourself with like-minded people, surround yourself with people who motivate you. Seek relationships with people whom you admire and aspire to be like. Befriend positive, hard-charging people. These people will help you become the person whom you want to be. The book of Proverbs supports the proposition that we can be positively shaped by the company we keep: "As iron sharpens iron, so man sharpens his fellow man."

Make no mistake – finding a superlative group of peers is no easy feat. As a busy, sometimes enervated young professional, you will feel a gravitational pull towards the sheer convenience and familiarity of your former peer group; but you must not fall into this trap. Set a realistic goal of hanging out with Taylor and Sam, who are more interested in drinking or smoking the night away than getting ahead in life, no more than twice per month; for all other times that you want (and need) human interaction, take a step outside of your comfort zone and pursue those who mirror the best, ideal version of you.

We all experience negative emotions and go through stressful, unfortunate periods of time in our life. None of us are perfect. In contrast with these normal, temporarily sidetracked people, negative people should be avoided like the plague. They drain your energy, one of the most precious resources you have.

Before I became an attorney, I had a "mentor" who I sought out for advice and guidance. He was a successful person, and a person whom I wanted to emulate. For some indecipherable reason, though, I frequently felt a loss of confidence and seemed to have lower self-esteem after meeting with him. For a couple of years, I convinced myself that he made me feel poorly because he was superior to me; i.e., he was so much more advanced that I felt dejected about how much progress I needed to make in my career. As I grew older and wiser, I realized that this person was unnecessarily causing my ill feelings. Rather than positively encouraging me, he fixated on the difficulties of my chosen journey. He planted seeds of doubt in the fertile soil that was my impressionable mind. He was nocuous.

Do not waste your time with people who consistently criticize, doubt, or demean you. They are robbers operating in the broad daylight, sometimes under the cowardly masquerade as mentors, with their sights set on your unavoidably fragile, positive energy. I am fond of the following quote by Mark Twain: "Keep away from people who belittle your ambitions. Small people always do that, but the really great make you feel that you, too, can become great." Bearing the foregoing in mind, do not shy away from people who – at appropriate times – provide you with constructive criticism. Excessively cheerful, or Pollyanna, people may not deliver to you the truth that you need.

Chapter 8: Not Taking Enough Risks [1]

Muhammad Ali, three-time world heavyweight champion, said that "He who is not courageous enough to take risks will accomplish nothing in life." He was right. One of the most damaging things you can do as a young professional is to be too cautious.

Financial advisors often recommend that young persons take bigger risks with their investments than older persons. They recommend more aggressive portfolios, ones that have a higher concentration of equity than debt securities. As a general rule of thumb, risk and reward are positively correlated. As young persons turn into older persons, their portfolios shift to holding more conservative positions – ones that are not as likely to result in a loss of principal, a potentially devastating consequence to individuals who need money for retirement or are unable to return to work.

Why is it, then, that many young people throw themselves at jobs with salaries hovering in the vicinity of $30,000? Adding insult to self-inflicted injury, young persons tend to give their employers carte blanche authority to control their lives.

I am aware that, in 2016, many students graduate with significant debt burdens. I have seen relatively current estimates of average undergraduate debt in excess of $35,000. Given the need for students to make payments on these loans, I can understand why recent graduates do not wish to become instant risk takers; nevertheless, I fail to see many graduates who, upon successfully retiring their loans, take calculated risks. They seem to have trained themselves to be reliant upon receiving a paycheck from their employers. Like programmed robots or planes on autopilot, these people operate without contemplation, fail to follow their passion, implicitly accept a life of servitude, and slowly erode the possibility of fulfilling their dreams.

James Carter, Jr., the 39th President of the United States, is quoted to have said the following: "Go out on a limb. That's where the fruit is." Regardless of your appetite for risk, you must understand that being successful requires more than accepting things as they are handed to you. You must seek to accomplish new feats and achieve higher goals.

For my first three years out of law school, I was an associate attorney at a well-respected, regional law firm. It was a prestigious position, one that roused envy from many of my peers. I had great clients, resources, and opportunities. By the time I was a second-year associate at the firm, I felt mostly the same way; but I began to question how much progress I was making. Was I gaining sufficient autonomy? Were my skills and rewards increasing fast enough?

Towards the end of that three-year period, I saw a lot of my peers – especially those who had gone into business for themselves – beginning to catch up with me. They had taken a few gambles, and some of them had paid off. While I still may have been ahead of some of them in the ultramarathon that is one's career, I could see that they were running much faster than me. It would not be long before they passed me, and, once they did, I would have no chance of catching up unless I changed my course. This gloomy realization was not consistent with my quest to follow 1 Corinthians 9:24: "Do you not know that the runners in the stadium all run in the race, but only one wins the prize? Run so as to win."

It took me three years to comprehend my former career trajectory. Looking back, I should have realized that – while my first attorney job was impressive – it did not require me to take many risks. My rewards were slow and incremental, and they would remain that way until I put some of my own skin in the game.

To understand why not taking enough risks is a common mistake, you must understand some behavioral economics. The concept of "loss aversion" refers to people's tendency to prefer the avoidance of a loss to the acquisition of a gain. The pain of losing is believed to be nearly twice as powerful as the pleasure of gaining. For example, a person who lost $50.00 would lose nearly twice the amount of psychological satisfaction as the amount he would gain by winning $50.00. Summarily stated, losses loom larger than gains; we like to win, but we *hate* to lose.

Within the context of a young professional's career, consideration of the penalty one could suffer because of failure predominates over the consideration of the reward one could enjoy because of success. Loss aversion, therefore, leads to risk aversion.

I learned about the concept of loss aversion while I was a student at the University of Kansas. It called to my attention how we can unwittingly, at times, make irrational decisions. My mere awareness of the concept has helped me to shed its effects. I hope that, within reason, you will experience similar results.

Even with your newfound knowledge of behavioral economics, if you are still scared of failing, I have a few other suggestions. Listen to Michael Jordan, arguably the greatest basketball player of all time: "I can accept failure. Everybody fails at something. But I can't accept not trying. Fear is an illusion." Alternatively, read Spencer Johnson's *Who Moved My Cheese* – one of my favorite quotes from which is "When you stop being afraid, you feel good!"

Here is a third, and more abstract, suggestion. Before you take President Carter's advice and begin crawling along your first limb, make sure it is the lowest, safest one. Crawl slowly, and take in your feelings all along the way. Keep your balance. Stretch and grasp the fruit. Carefully make your way back to the trunk of the tree, and take your time dismounting it. Then, give yourself some positive reinforcement: eat the fruit immediately. After you have consumed every last ounce of it, resolve to never indulge in something that sweet again without earning it. Shun the delicacies with which the merchants try to entice you. You are now a hunter (a modern and vegan one, that is), programmed to reward yourself after you have profited. Begin aiming for higher limbs, and traverse them with greater confidence.

You will soon find yourself many feet above where you started and stories above those who never tried. They now look up to you with great admiration.

Chapter 9: Neglecting Your Health

Your health is the most important asset that you have. It should be guarded as carefully as the United States Government guards Fort Knox, and as frequently too – 24 hours a day. Without good health, you will struggle immensely to advance your career.

Some of us have ailments. We were born with them or developed them over time. There is no shame in not being the picture of health if we make the best out of what we have been given or what we have now.

With varying degrees of severity, I have seen young professionals unintentionally maraud their health for the glory of their companies. The habits that you form in the beginning of your career will be hard to break. Never, ever get in the habit of neglecting your health. If you are like me – and believe that this life is the only one you will ever have – or, at the very least, do not want to chance having a living existence beyond what you presently know, you should almost always service your body and your mind ahead of the needs of your company.

Eating a proper diet and exercising regularly are two of the mainstays for mental and physical health. Each of us has different abilities and restrictions. Visit with your doctor about designing a workout routine and what (and how much) you should be eating.

John F. Kennedy, the 35th President of the United States, remarked that "Physical fitness is not only one of the most important keys to a healthy body, it is the basis of dynamic and creative intellectual ability." On the other side of the aisle, George W. Bush, the 43rd President of the United States, echoed President Kennedy's belief: "There's never a question in my mind that I'll exercise. Even when I travel, there's always a treadmill in my room. I have a treadmill on Air Force One."

There is no excuse, other than your doctor's orders, for not exercising. Many of us work in multi-story office buildings. If you are fortunate enough to work above the first floor, take the stairs. After walking up them to report to work, down them to get lunch, up them to report back to work, and down them to return home, you have made nice progress towards your daily physical fitness goals. Use your legs to initiate communication rather than your fingers. You will burn a lot more calories, and give your mind a much needed respite, if you walk down the hall to visit with a colleague instead of pecking keys on a keyboard or dialing intra-office extensions. Stand up. You often do not need to think or speak in your chair. Sitting for extended periods of time wreaks havoc on our backs. Occasionally trade your traditional desk chair out for a core-strengthening stability ball. If you do not mind your coworkers thinking you are a little "different," do some light shadow boxing – throw a punch or two into the air, but make sure that nobody is around first!

Hippocrates, a physician from ancient Greece who is regarded as the father of medicine, said to "Let food be thy medicine and medicine be thy food." While the importance of modern medicine and pharmaceuticals cannot be denied, neither can the truth of Hippocrates' message.

Foods have healing properties. We eat them to obtain sufficient amounts of the three primary macronutrients – fat, protein, and carbohydrate. These provide us with the energy, in the form of calories, that we need to function at our jobs. How much of each a person needs is dependent upon age, gender, weight, muscle mass, and activity level. Related to macronutrients is the concept of essential nutrients. They include all three macronutrients as well as vitamins, minerals, and water. Without them, we cannot live. A third category is phytonutrients. They are not essential to our survival, but they are essential to the quality of our health. Found primarily in fruits and vegetables, phytonutrients help build a strong immune system, prevent disease, and keep your body functioning normally.

Dieticians frequently recommend that we eat whole foods. What does that mean? It means that we should be eating foods that are unprocessed and unrefined. These foods are easy to recognize – they should look the same or very similar to how they did when existing in nature. Given the essential nutrient and phytonutrient differences amongst foods and our potential to get bored with a limited diet, dieticians also recommend that we eat a variety of foods. They also recommend that we pay attention to our portions and try not to consume added sugar.

Eating the perfect diet is time-consuming and requires immense discipline, and most of us do not want to put forth the commensurate effort. Let me address one common, work-oriented mistake I see young persons make that would require minimal effort to correct: making the wrong lunch choices.

Most of us enjoy going out to lunch. It allows us to leave the office and socialize, two very important activities for long-term success. Over time, though, we get busy, and we search for lunch options that are expedient. Young persons conflate food that can be purchased and eaten quickly with fast food. They are not the same. Options exist besides calorically dense pizza, trans fat-laden cheeseburgers, and preservative-packed hot dogs. What are some of these options? One is Whole Foods Market, an American supermarket chain that sells minimally processed foods free of hydrogenated fats and artificial additives. A person can select his meal of choice from a smorgasbord of hot and cold food offerings, including salads, fruits, and prepared, seasoned meats. Another example is Chipotle Mexican Grill, which probably needs no introduction. At Chipotle, a young person can enjoy a burrito bowl with healthy ingredients such as brown rice, black beans, fajita vegetables – green bell peppers and red onions, guacamole, lettuce, and a choice of a "responsibly raised" meat, which comes from an animal that has not been genetically modified. At either of these places, healthy food can be eaten quickly, cheaply, and in the company of your choice.

If you are too busy or simply do not wish to go out to lunch, I have another suggestion: bring a homemade smoothie or blended shake. I have been doing this for well over a decade and cannot emphasize enough how much time, money, and doctors visits it has saved me. Making a smoothie or blended shake is more of an art than a science, but I will share with you what has worked for me. I put up to six essential ingredients in a blender – a seed, an oil, a vegetable, a protein, a fruit, and a butter. Three of the healthiest foods on the planet are flaxseeds, chia seeds, and hemp seeds. Choose one of them. For an oil, use MCT or flax. With respect to the vegetable component, opt for a leafy green – either kale, spinach, or arugula. Protein is most easily added in the form of a powder, which can be dairy based (whey or casein), egg based, or plant based (soy, rice, pea, or hemp). The fruit can be nearly any type, but I commonly use apples or berries. The best butter choices are almond or peanut. After adding one ingredient from three or more of the different categories to my blender, I run it for at least two cycles (which takes two minutes, at most). The result is creamy, smooth, sometimes tasty but always bizarrely colored liquid medicine! Mix and match your own ingredients, and do not feel compelled to make a shake as "unique" as mine.

Eating well not only improves the quality of your physical health but also your mental health, which is of utmost importance. An alarming 50 million people within the United States alone experience mental illness in a given year. Besides diet and exercise, there are a handful of generally accepted techniques for improving your mental health. Two easy ones to remember are getting enough sleep and *timely* light exposure each day.

When I began my career, I almost always took my cell phone or iPad with me to bed. I would use one or the other to browse the Internet, check social media, and obsessively monitor my work email inbox. If I received an important email during this bedtime routine, my mind would become alert and enter into problem-solving mode. It would take me at least an hour, possibly much longer, to cool this adrenaline response. To make matters worse, I was inhibiting the production of the sleep-inducing hormone melatonin by staring into the blue light emitted by my screen. The result was a shifting of my body's natural clock to later and later hours in the evening, which could only be partially offset by later starts to my work day.

It took me years to realize that this routine was foolish. Nearly every email I received after 5:30 PM did not concern an urgent matter or, if it did, could not be appropriately addressed until the following morning. Unless a person is in the medical profession or a member of an emergency personnel team or service unit, he or she probably does not have any exigent business to handle in the evenings. And the blue light I was absorbing in bed, even if it was not for the purpose of handling emails, was needlessly costly and easily fixable. I learned (and continue to implement today) that I could change the display settings on my device such that the colors were inverted or in grayscale. (Other light reduction techniques can be used as well, such as wearing light-filtering glasses or installing specialized software on your device(s).

If you have been neglecting your health to date, then do not worry; heed the following Chinese proverb: "The best time to plant a tree was 20 years ago. The second best time is now."

Chapter 10: Failing To Build Your Brand

Do you have anybody, besides yourself (and possibly your mother), who promotes you? Are your coworkers good about recognizing your accomplishments? Does your marketing officer or coordinator make your personal successes known? If you answered "No" to any of these questions, or even all three of them, you are not alone.

When you first begin your job, you may enjoy new relationship energy – colloquially described as the "honeymoon phase." You are excited about being part of a new company, meeting new people, having more responsibility, and earning a paycheck. You are fully engaged in your job and very much enjoy your role on the company's team.

Chances are that, after six months, these feelings will wear off. You will realize that your company has flaws and asymmetries, just as every other company does. Chances are also that, less than four years (or potentially far sooner) after this epiphany you will have transitioned to another job. With the frequency of job changes made today, your old employer will not bear the burden of providing you a proper funeral: unless you illegally damaged the company's business interests, you will be unceremoniously cremated and forgotten in an instant.

Companies have become shrewd. Why would they build your brand when you may not be with them in a few years? Some companies believe, therefore, that promoting their individual employees is, simply, a bad investment. The company has staying power. The employees do not.

You should now apprehend, unequivocally, that you need to invest in yourself and build your brand. Ideally, you should be building your brand while simultaneously building your company's. (See Chapter 4.) If you merely focus on building your personal brand, you may be asked to leave. If you merely focus on building your company's brand, you have done the equivalent of casting your paddles overboard and entrusting the one-way river to deliver you to the promised land (found upstream).

Do not consign yourself to being a paddleless rower. Instead, take an active role in the establishment of your professional identity. How do you do this? There are two primary techniques. Each one, when pursued separately, will generate results. When pursued in concert, the two techniques have a synergistic, or at least additive, effect.

The late Napoleon Hill, a famous author and an advisor to former United States Presidents Woodrow Wilson and Franklin Roosevelt, proclaimed that "It is literally true that you can succeed best and quickest by helping others to succeed." In essence, success is a two-step process: step number one is helping other people; step number two is allowing the people you have helped to become your helpers. This prescription for success could not be more true for a friend of mine who I will call "George."

When I was in law school and graduate business school, 2008 to 2012, the nation's economy was in terrible shape. The legal economy mirrored, at best, the nation's economy. I knew that the ticket to permanent placement (in a law firm) was through securing one or more summer clerkships. George was three years my senior. He had passed the bar exam and was on his way to building his practice. I hardly knew anything else about George; however, for a reason not completely clear to me in hindsight, I mustered up the courage to cold-call him. Despite my hopes that I may be able to leave a voicemail, George answered the phone in a deep, intimidating voice. As succinctly as possible, I told him that I was a budding attorney, that I briefly knew of him, and that I would be obliged if he would meet me for lunch sometime within the month near his office. To my surprise, he verbally agreed to meet me for lunch.

A few weeks later, George and I had lunch. I had questions, and George had answers. After George's generous supply of information and absorption of the bill, I had the gall to ask him about employment. He said that he could not afford to hire me. I understood. After all, George was just getting his own practice off the ground. Instead of leaving the conversation at that, George told me that he knew of others who may be able to hire me for a summer clerkship and that he would introduce me to them.

George made good on his word. He introduced me to a group of attorneys that extended me a job offer for the upcoming summer. I ultimately declined that job offer and accepted another, but that did not alter the gratitude I had stored up for George.

Years later, when my legal career had begun to flourish, I continued to hold George in high regard. I felt compelled to return the favor he did for me, but I wondered how I could do so. He did not need a job; he did not need my advice; and he did not need my company. The answer haphazardly presented itself to me when an individual arrived at my office seeking representation. We were unable to help her, yet she still needed legal assistance. At that moment, I realized that I could not only direct her to the hands of a capable attorney but could repay the debt, with interest, that I had owed to my dear friend George. The woman called George, retained him, and was ultimately awarded a jury verdict. George could not have been more pleased with me. That referral was the first of over a dozen that I sent to George.

While the story of me and George is powerful, you need to be familiar with the second, and more direct, technique of establishing your professional identity. It is not complicated to understand, but it is difficult to execute. Simply stated, the second technique is self-promotion.

People have difficulty self-promoting because they do not want to be viewed as braggarts or egotists. If you are one of these people, I challenge you to analyze your daily activities and determine whether some of them are or are not, intentionally or otherwise, befitting of the characteristics of your intended antithesis. Do you write Facebook posts about having enjoyed a nice meal, run a certain distance, or attended a popular sporting event? Do you tweet about having earned a good grade, landed a good job, or won over a good client? Do you use Instagram to show your followers the luxuries of your vacation spot? Off the social media spectrum, do you cheer for your alma mater and against your alma mater's rivals? All of these actions, viewed in a vacuum, can be classified as selfish, braggadocios, or egotistical behavior. If you are going to engage in self-promotional behavior, why not make it productive? Here are three exemplary ways to do so: (1) write articles for respected publications that demonstrate your command of applicable subject matter; (2) give extracurricular presentations concerning impending changes in your field; or (3) do excellent work, and make sure that its results are made known to decision-makers.

In 2009, Gary Vaynerchuk made a bold prediction in his book *Crush It!*: "Mark my words, if you want to stay relevant and competitive in the coming years – I don't care if you're in sales, tech, finance, publishing, journalism, event planning, business development, retail, service, you name it – you will still need to develop and grow your personal brand." He was right. Gone are the days when a person could comfortably exist as an unidentified brick exterior to his company's framework. You must personally become a known commodity, or, even better, a known necessity.